Original title:
New Habits

Author: Tim Wood
ISBN HARDBACK: 978-9916-88-288-7
ISBN PAPERBACK: 978-9916-88-289-4

Celestial Compass

Stars above, a guiding light,
Whispering secrets of the night.
Winds that carry dreams untold,
Navigating hearts, brave and bold.

Constellations share their lore,
Charting paths to distant shores.
In the silence, hope takes flight,
As we wander through the night.

Reaching for the Unwritten

Pages blank, a tale awaits,
Ink in hand, unlock the gates.
Fingers dance on empty space,
Crafting worlds with hope and grace.

Words unfurl like blossoms bright,
Flourishing in morning light.
Every heartbeat, every sigh,
Ripples echo, dreams comply.

Radiance of Renewal

Morning glows in amber hues,
Nature's canvas, fresh and new.
Time to shed the weight we bear,
Embrace the warmth, the kisses rare.

Petals open, colors bloom,
In our hearts, dispelling gloom.
Life reborn, each moment flows,
In this light, our spirit grows.

Cumulus Clouds of Change

Fluffy shapes against the blue,
Whispers of the winds break through.
Shifting softly, drifting high,
Echoing the dreams that fly.

Raindrops fall, sweet serenade,
Cleansing hearts, the past will fade.
Beneath the clouds, we stand as one,
Embracing change, a new begun.

Embers of Determination

From ash and flame, we rise anew,
Each setback fuels the fire in you.
With heart ablaze, we forge our way,
In darkest night, we'll find our day.

Through obstacles, our spirits soar,
Each challenge met, we seek for more.
With grit and grace, we push ahead,
For in our hearts, the fire is fed.

Legends of Liminality

In twilight's glow, we find our fate,
Between the worlds, we hesitate.
A whisper calls from realms unknown,
In this still space, strength has grown.

To dance on edges, brave and bold,
In moments fleeting, tales unfold.
We are the dreams that dare to stray,
In shadows cast, we'll light our way.

Sowing Seeds of Development

With gentle hands, we plant the seeds,
In fertile grounds, we grow our deeds.
Each thought a sprout, each task a thread,
Together woven, paths we tread.

Through trials faced, the roots run deep,
In healthy soil, our visions leap.
As future blooms from present's grace,
We nurture dreams in this safe space.

Unraveling Threads

In tangled webs, we find the truth,
With careful hands and hearts of youth.
Each strand reveals a story spun,
In threads we trace, our journey's begun.

With patience born of time's embrace,
We seek the pattern, find our place.
In every knot, a lesson learned,
As one by one, the threads are turned.

Embracing the Unfamiliar

In shadows where the wild winds blow,
New paths emerge where few may go.
Each step a chance, each glance anew,
Embrace the change, let courage brew.

The echoes of doubt whisper near,
Yet in the heart, we quell the fear.
With every dawn, the courage grows,
In the unknown, true strength shows.

Every Day a Canvas

The morning light spills golden bright,
A canvas born from shade to light.
Brush strokes of hope in colors bold,
Each day a story yet untold.

With every choice, the hues we blend,
A masterpiece that has no end.
Life's palette rich, the colors sway,
Every moment, a brand new day.

Steps into the Unknown

With hesitant feet on paths unseen,
We forge ahead, both brave and keen.
Through fog and doubt, the road unfolds,
Each step we take, a tale retold.

The stars above, they guide the way,
In silence found, we choose to stay.
Trusting the journey, come what may,
We dance with fate, come night or day.

The Rhythm of Reinvention

In cycles worn, we feel the beat,
A dance of change beneath our feet.
With every turn, a new refrain,
In rhythms fresh, we break the chain.

The past will whisper, call our name,
Yet forward steps ignite the flame.
Transforming self, we find our song,
In endless flow, where we belong.

Mosaic of Intentions

Each thought a piece, a vibrant hue,
We gather moments, both old and new.
With every choice, a shape we find,
A canvas formed, reflections bind.

In kindness' thread, we weave our fate,
A tapestry rich, we cultivate.
Through trials faced, our spirits rise,
In this mosaic, our truth lies.

From dreams once whispered, plans take flight,
A symphony of purpose shines bright.
With open hearts, we craft our day,
A masterpiece born from the clay.

In future's grasp, our visions soar,
United by hopes, we seek for more.
A dance of souls, with passion's flare,
In this mosaic, we all share.

Dreams in Motion

Awake in night's embrace we chase,
The fleeting dreams, a sacred space.
With eyes aglow, we dare to leap,
Into the depths where wishes sleep.

Through starlit paths, we wander free,
With every turn, a new decree.
Hearts in sync, like rivers flow,
Together bound, we ebb and glow.

In whispered winds, our hopes take flight,
Carving stories in soft moonlight.
Each step a dance on life's grand stage,
We write our tales, page by page.

As dawn unfolds, potential gleams,
Awakening the brightened dreams.
With courage found, we boldly steer,
In dreams of motion, we persevere.

Constellations of Change

In the night's vast, we gaze above,
Each star a beacon, whispers of love.
From darkness, light begins to bloom,
A map of hope to dispel the gloom.

Guiding us through the winds of fate,
Constellations shift, we resonate.
In silent storms, our spirits bend,
With every trial, new paths ascend.

Embracing shifts as seasons turn,
Fractals of time, we learn and yearn.
In every change, a clearer view,
A cosmic dance, forever true.

So let us chart our journey bold,
With dreams ignited, stories told.
In constellations, we find our way,
A tapestry bright, come what may.

The Journey Within

In silence deep, I seek my soul,
Through winding paths, I become whole.
Each step I take, a breath anew,
A light within that guides me through.

In shadows cast, my fears arise,
Yet hope ignites, a flame that flies.
With every thought, I pave my way,
Unraveling dreams that gently sway.

Through tangled thoughts, I find my peace,
With every yearning, doubts do cease.
The journey in, a sacred rite,
To discover depths and inner light.

Through whispers soft, the truth I find,
In the silent corners of my mind.
Each heartbeat echoes, a song divine,
On this journey deep, my spirit shines.

Shadows of the Future

In twilight's glow, the shadows dance,
They weave a tale of fate and chance.
Whispers of dreams yet to unfold,
In shadows cast, our hopes are bold.

A canvas blank, with colors bright,
The future calls, wrapped in the night.
Mysteries lie in every shade,
Timid hearts may be afraid.

Yet courage stirs in silent hearts,
In shadows deep, a spark imparts.
To chase the light through every doubt,
And break the fears that linger out.

Together we walk, hands intertwined,
Chasing the visions in our mind.
With every step, the shadows fade,
A brighter dawn, the moment made.

Carving New Landscapes

With chisel firm, I shape the stone,
A vision born, my heart has grown.
Each stroke a promise, each line a dream,
In rugged terrain, I carve and glean.

The mountains rise, the valleys show,
A new horizon where rivers flow.
In nature's hands, my craft unfolds,
A tapestry of life retold.

Through storms and calm, my spirit seeks,
The beauty found in daring peaks.
Each landscape drawn, a story wakes,
In sacred earth, my journey takes.

These curves and bends, my heart's embrace,
In every curve, I find my place.
The world transformed by hands so bold,
A legacy of dreams retold.

Quests for Clarity

Through tangled thickets, I pursue,
A quest for truth beneath the dew.
Each question asked, a pathway wide,
In search of answers, I must glide.

With every doubt, my compass spins,
Discovering where the journey begins.
The fog may linger in quiet streams,
Yet hope ignites the brightest dreams.

In moments still, the echoes call,
To rise and shine, to break the fall.
Through trials faced, I gain my sight,
In shadows deep, I seek the light.

Connected souls in this vast sea,
With clarity shared, we learn to be.
Each step we take, a bond renewed,
In quests for clarity, love imbued.

Unfolding Dreams

In whispers soft, the night draws near,
A canvas wide, where hopes appear.
Each star a spark, a wish in flight,
Unfolding dreams in silver light.

With gentle hands, we shape the dawn,
A promise made, a new day born.
Through valleys deep and hills that gleam,
We chase the threads of every dream.

The heart beats loud, a steady drum,
In rhythm with the dreams we hum.
The journey long, the path unclear,
Yet every step is filled with cheer.

In unity, our voices rise,
To weave the truth beneath the skies.
With every breath, we find our way,
Unfolding dreams, come what may.

The Sound of Solitude

In quiet moments, shadows blend,
The world outside begins to bend.
A whisper soft, the heart's refrain,
The sound of solitude, its gain.

With every breath, the silence speaks,
In gentle waves, as stillness seeks.
A hidden space where thoughts can roam,
In solitude, we find our home.

The echoes dance, a soft embrace,
In tranquil time, we find our place.
Through whispered dreams, we let them flow,
The sound of solitude, we know.

In moonlit nights, reflections gleam,
A canvas wide, we start to dream.
With every sigh, a tale unfolds,
The sound of solitude, it holds.

Bridges to Tomorrow

Across the river, strong and wide,
We build our dreams with hope as guide.
Each step we take, a bridge anew,
To span the gaps to what is true.

With open hearts, we pave the way,
For brighter lives that greet the day.
Through storms we march, through winds so strong,
These bridges lead where we belong.

In unity, we rise as one,
Together bound until we've won.
Through every trial, we will stand,
Creating paths, hand in hand.

With visions clear, we see the light,
A future bright, within our sight.
These bridges built, our dreams will soar,
To carry us to evermore.

Echoes of Purpose

In the stillness, voices call,
Echoes of purpose, we won't fall.
With every step, a story shared,
In unity, our hearts prepared.

Through trials faced, we find our way,
In whispered truths, we learn to stay.
The weight we carry, light as air,
Echoes of purpose, beyond compare.

With eyes aglow, we chase the dawn,
In every shadow, the light is drawn.
These echoes linger, strong and clear,
A guiding force, forever near.

Together we forge, together we rise,
With dreams as vast as endless skies.
In every heartbeat, life we trace,
Echoes of purpose, we embrace.

Tiny Triumphs

In whispers of dawn, hope takes flight,
Small victories spark in the soft morning light.
Each step we take, each smile we share,
A tapestry woven with love and care.

A child's first laugh, a friend's gentle touch,
Moments that matter, they mean so much.
In simple joys, true wealth we find,
Tiny triumphs, a treasure entwined.

Bright petals unfurl, a flower in bloom,
Casting away shadows, dispelling the gloom.
Celebrate each heartbeat, each cheer, each sigh,
For the little things teach us how to fly.

In the garden of life, sow seeds of delight,
Nurture them gently, let love ignite.
Tiny triumphs remind us to see,
The beauty in moments, so precious and free.

Awakening Momentum

Morning breaks with a whispering breeze,
Awakening dreams with effortless ease.
The world stirs to life, vibrant and bright,
Fueled by the magic of emerging light.

Steps on the pavement, a rhythm unfolds,
Stories of courage and strength retold.
Hearts intertwine as paths intertwine,
A dance of connection, a lifeline divine.

Lifted by purpose, we gather our might,
Chasing the shadows, embracing the light.
Momentum builds, a wave of desire,
With every heartbeat, we fuel the fire.

Together we rise, together we stand,
Crafting the future, hand in hand.
Each moment we claim, each dream we ignite,
We carry the spark, we are the light.

Rebirth in the Everyday

In the hum of the city, life swells anew,
Every sunrise paints skies with a different hue.
A moment of stillness in the chaos we chase,
Rebirth in the everyday, a gentle embrace.

Fading shadows echo the past we have known,
Yet hope is the seed that is courageously sown.
Amidst the routine, magic resides,
In laughter of friends and love that collides.

The rust of routine, brushed away with care,
Fresh eyes to behold, in the mundane we share.
With each breath taken, springs forth a new day,
Awakening wonders that guide our way.

Rebirth in the moments, unwrapped like a gift,
In daily encounters, our spirits uplift.
Embrace the ordinary, for therein we find,
Life's quiet miracles, beautifully intertwined.

Lanterns of Reflection

In twilight's embrace, lanterns softly glow,
Illuminating paths where the heart longs to go.
Each flickering flame tells a tale of the past,
Lessons learned tenderly, shadows cast.

Reflecting on journeys, both near and afar,
Guided by light, like a soft shining star.
In the stillness we ponder, in silence we hear,
The whispers of wisdom, both gentle and clear.

Lanterns of memories, flickering bright,
Echoing laughter, and warming the night.
Each glow is a story, each beam holds a dream,
The fabric of life, intricately weaved seam.

As darkness surrounds, let the lanterns ignite,
Hope in the distance, dispelling the night.
Together we gather, in love we connect,
Forging a future with lanterns of reflection.

The Pulse of Progress

In the heart where dreams ignite,
Innovation takes its flight.
Paths once dark, now filled with light,
Human spirit, bold and bright.

Brick by brick, we build the way,
Nothing lost, yet all to gain.
Voices rise, together sway,
A future painted, free from pain.

Change the rhythm, feel the beat,
With every step, our hopes repeat.
Like a drum, we march in sync,
In unity, we find the link.

Through the struggles, through despair,
The pulse of progress fills the air.
In every heart, in every hand,
We forge ahead, together stand.

Choices Etched in Time

Every moment, a fork in the road,
Paths diverge, with each heavy load.
Whispers call, the future unknown,
In each pause, seeds of fate are sown.

Choices linger like shadows, it's true,
Every step shapes the life we pursue.
Weighing the options, heart on the line,
In the silence, decisions entwine.

Looking back, the echoes remind,
Of laughter shared, moments unkind.
Through joy and sorrow, we learn to see,
Choices forged, we set ourselves free.

In the tapestry of days gone by,
Our choices gleam, like stars in the sky.
Etched in time, their stories unfold,
Creating wisdom, more precious than gold.

Embracing the Unknown

With open arms, we face the night,
In shadows dark, we seek the light.
Adventures call, a daring quest,
Embracing fear, we rise, we rest.

The path is blurred, yet hearts ignite,
In uncertain trails, we find our might.
In every twist, a chance to learn,
Embracing change, our spirits burn.

Trust the journey, trust the flow,
In the unknown, we rise and grow.
Believe the call, let courage steer,
In the vastness, we conquer fear.

In every heartbeat, whispers play,
A melody guiding the way.
Through the mist, new dreams we find,
In embracing all, we leave fear behind.

Blooming in the Moment

In petals soft, a story unfolds,
Moments cherished, like treasures of gold.
With colors bright, life's canvas displayed,
In every heart, love's gentle cascade.

Catch the sunrise, feel its warm kiss,
In fleeting time, we find our bliss.
Each second is a chance to grow,
In every smile, let tenderness show.

Listen closely, the whispers of now,
Breathe in deeply, feel the vow.
To cherish today, this gift we keep,
In blooms of joy, our souls leap.

Dance with laughter, sway with the breeze,
In every moment, life aims to please.
Bloom where you are, let colors swell,
In the present, our stories dwell.

Rituals in Silence

In quiet corners, shadows play,
Whispers of wisdom drift away,
Moments held in gentle grace,
Time pauses in this sacred space.

Candles flicker, shadows dance,
Heartbeats echo in the trance,
Breath of stillness, peace profound,
In the silence, truth is found.

The world outside can fade away,
In these rituals, here we stay,
Listening deeply to the soul,
Unveiling secrets, making whole.

Stepping softly, we explore,
Each silence opens up a door,
Connection blooms in quiet's sway,
In these rituals, we find our way.

Winds of Growth

Gentle breezes stir the leaves,
Nature's hymn, a sweet reprieve,
Roots extend beneath the ground,
In this dance, new life is found.

With every gust, a change begins,
Seeds of promise in soft spins,
Branches reach for skies above,
In the winds, we feel the love.

Patience taught through moments still,
Nature's rhythm, quiet will,
As seasons shift, our hearts align,
In the winds, our dreams entwine.

Embrace the growth, let go of fear,
Winds will carry, loud and clear,
Together, we can rise and soar,
In the winds of growth, we explore.

Shifting Sands

Beneath the sun, the grains do shift,
Time's embrace, a gentle gift,
Footprints fade with the tide's return,
In shifting sands, we live and learn.

Whispers call from distant shores,
As the ocean shares its roars,
Ephemeral, yet so profound,
In these sands, our stories bound.

Every moment, fleeting fast,
Echoes of a world amassed,
Waves of change, they carve and mold,
In shifting sands, our lives unfold.

So let us dance upon this stage,
Embrace the flux, turn every page,
For in this journey, we expand,
Together in the shifting sands.

The Call of Potential

In the stillness, a voice arises,
Hinting at hidden, vast surprises,
Feel the pull, a gentle thread,
It beckons softly, moves ahead.

Dreams awaken, shadows fade,
Seeds of promise, gently laid,
Whispers linger in the air,
The call of potential, always there.

Each heartbeat echoes, strong and true,
Guiding steps to what we can do,
With courage found within our core,
We answer boldly, seek for more.

Embrace the journey, trust the way,
Let hope and passion light the day,
For every soul has a story told,
In the call of potential, bright and bold.

Harvesting Moments

Time slips softly through our hands,
Gathering whispers of the land.
Each second, ripe with hope and dreams,
Weave the fabric of our schemes.

Golden fields under the sun,
Moments shared, two become one.
Collecting laughter, saving tears,
A treasure built across the years.

In the silence, we will find,
The echoes of our hearts aligned.
Harvesting all that life imparts,
Planting seeds within our hearts.

Together in this fleeting light,
Capturing day, embracing night.
For in the moments that we share,
Lies the beauty of our care.

Spirals of Intent

In the dance of thoughts we spin,
Circles widen, deep within.
Intentions crafted with our hands,
Guiding futures, shifting sands.

Each layer forms a story told,
Whispers of the brave and bold.
With every twist, we carve our way,
Through the night and into day.

Dreams ascend like smoke on air,
Spirals weave the burdens bare.
We rise and fall, a sacred rite,
Finding strength in shared insight.

With purpose clear, we move ahead,
Every path begins with tread.
In the spirals, we become,
An endless dance, forever spun.

Cascades of Growth

From tiny seeds, great trees will rise,
Reaching upward, towards the skies.
Roots entwined in earth below,
In silent strength, they learn to grow.

Each drop of rain, a gentle kiss,
Nurturing dreams, a dance of bliss.
Petals open to the sun,
Cascades burst forth, life's begun.

In the garden, time weaves slow,
Growth contained in every row.
Seasons change, but still we thrive,
In the richness, we survive.

Connected to the world around,
In every layer, growth is found.
Nature's pulse within our veins,
Cascades of life, where hope remains.

Light Through the Cracks

Shadows linger, dark and deep,
In quiet corners, secrets keep.
Yet from the gaps where light spills through,
A promise of the fresh and new.

Finding beauty in the flaws,
Nature's art, without a cause.
Each fracture tells its own sweet tale,
Of strength that rises, will not fail.

Through the cracks, we glimpse the sky,
Hope ignites, and spirits fly.
In fractured moments, wisdom grows,
Light reveals what darkness knows.

So let us cherish every seam,
For in the cracks, life finds its gleam.
With every ray that breaks the night,
We discover our own light.

Tides of Transformation

Waves crash and recede, a dance of fate,
In the ebbing rhythm, we hesitate.
With each new tide, old weights release,
Emerging stronger, finding peace.

The moon pulls softly at our core,
Guiding us home to distant shores.
In this fluid motion, we grow wide,
With every heartbeat, we coincide.

Shells shift on sands, stories untold,
In whispers of water, dreams unfold.
Transformation flows, the heart aligns,
In this vast ocean, true self shines.

With courage, we ride the waves of change,
Embracing the unknown, we rearrange.
Each splash a promise, each swell a sign,
In tides of transformation, we redefine.

Whispered Resolutions

In silent corners, dreams take flight,
Softly whispered in the night.
Secrets wrapped in hopeful tones,
Resolutions dance on whispered bones.

In twilight's glow, intentions bloom,
Casting shadows in the room.
With every breath, we hold our vow,
To nurture whispers, here and now.

The heart recalls each silent plea,
Navigating through what could be.
With gentle steps, we brave the call,
Reaching higher, lest we fall.

Time bends softly, moments fade,
In whispered resolutions, dreams cascade.
We weave our paths with threads of light,
Embracing the dawn that ends the night.

Seeds of Tomorrow

In soil rich, we plant our hopes,
Tiny seeds with vast scopes.
Nurtured dreams in sun's embrace,
Growth unfurls at its own pace.

Gentle rains whisper their vows,
Caressing earth, feeding brows.
From tiny whispers, life will thrive,
In each small seed, the will to strive.

Roots dig deep, anchoring soul,
In the garden, we find our role.
Hope grows tall, reaching the skies,
In the heart of every sunrise.

With time, the blooms will fill our days,
Each petal holds a thousand ways.
In seeds of tomorrow, we find our song,
As together we rise, united and strong.

Uncharted Paths

On unmarked trails, we tread the day,
With every step, we find our way.
Footprints linger in the dust,
Faithful hearts, in dreams we trust.

The horizon calls with a vibrant hue,
A journey painted fresh and new.
With courage bright, we face the sun,
In uncharted paths, we're never done.

Winding roads and whispers low,
Guide our spirits where to go.
Each turn reveals a hidden prize,
In the adventure, our spirit flies.

With laughter, we embrace the wild,
Every moment, a wandering child.
Exploring realms where dreams entwine,
On uncharted paths, our hearts align.

The Art of Reinvention

In shadows cast by dreams we've chased,
We find the strength to leave the past.
A canvas blank, our hopes embraced,
With every stroke, our spirits fast.

We twist and bend, reshape our fate,
Through trials lost, we learn to soar.
Each heartbeat tells, we cultivate,
A journey rich with tales galore.

Embracing change, we shed the skin,
With courage bold, we face the dawn.
In every loss, a chance to win,
A brighter self, reborn, redrawn.

So let the winds of fortune guide,
The path to dreams we dare explore.
In art of life, we take our stride,
Reinvented now, forevermore.

Morning Rituals

The sun peeks in, a gentle light,
With whispered calm, the day awakes.
A sip of tea, the world feels right,
In quietude, the heart partakes.

Stretching limbs as night recedes,
Breath by breath, the spirit soars.
In stillness found, the mind concedes,
New dreams arise, behind closed doors.

A glance outside at nature's grace,
Birds take flight, the skies alive.
In simple joys, we find our place,
In morning's hush, our hopes revive.

With gratitude, we face the day,
Embracing all that life imparts.
These morning rituals gently lay,
Foundations strong within our hearts.

Echoes of Intention

In whispered thoughts that fill the air,
Our intentions take their flight.
With purpose sharp, we dare to care,
And manifest the dreamer's light.

Each step we take, a path designed,
With clarity, our souls align.
Through struggles faced, we seek to find,
The echoes of a love divine.

A vision clear, the future bright,
With open hearts, we pave the way.
In every choice, we chase the light,
Echoes guide us, day by day.

So trust the tune that life will play,
For every note, a story weaves.
With hearts in tune, come what may,
Our echoes dance in dreamlike eaves.

Fragments of Routine

In quiet rhythm, moments blend,
The tick of time, a steady beat.
Each fragment stitched, as days ascend,
In usual paths, the mind finds heat.

The fragrance of coffee fills the space,
While sunlight spills on wooden floors.
In hurried steps, we find our pace,
A comfort found in open doors.

Yet within the mundane lies the art,
In every glance, a world anew.
We capture magic, the simplest part,
In fragments, life opens its view.

So cherish patterns woven tight,
For even routine holds the vast.
In daily acts, from morn to night,
Fragments scatter, echoes cast.

Beyond Comfort's Edge

In shadows deep where silence dwells,
The heartbeats quicken, fear compels.
A step beyond the known embrace,
A world awakened, space to chase.

The edge of comfort, sharp and bright,
Calls forth the courage, ignites the light.
With every stride, the doubts take flight,
To venture forth into the night.

Paths untraveled, whispers heard,
In the stillness, freedom stirred.
Beyond the walls of soft retreat,
Adventure lies in daring feet.

With every breath, the spirit soars,
Unearthing dreams on distant shores.
Beyond comfort's grasp, we dare to find,
The truths concealed within the mind.

The Echo of Promise

In distant echoes, dreams collide,
Promises made, no place to hide.
Each whisper holds a secret thought,
In every heart, a lesson taught.

With time, the shadows start to part,
A melody plays within the heart.
The journey calls, the path is clear,
Hope dances close, it's drawing near.

We chase the songs of what could be,
In every sigh, a symphony.
The echo lingers, soft yet bold,
A story waiting to unfold.

Through tangled woods, the light will gleam,
In every struggle, find the dream.
For in the echo, whispers say,
A promise waits to light the way.

Threads of Transformation

We weave our tales with threads of time,
In vibrant hues, a rhythm, a rhyme.
Stitching moments, a tapestry bright,
Crafting change in the fabric of light.

Each knot a lesson, each loop a turn,
In every heart, the fire will burn.
Unraveling fears, we learn to stand,
With open hearts and steady hands.

As seasons shift and colors fade,
A new design is lovingly laid.
For every ending births a start,
Threads of transformation bind the heart.

In woven paths, the future sings,
Emerging strength in fragile wings.
Through every change, we learn and grow,
In threads of life, the essence flows.

Fragments of the Future

In glimpses caught, the future gleams,
A fractured lens through which it seems.
Each fragment holds a piece of light,
A puzzle formed of day and night.

With every choice, a path unfolds,
In whispered dreams, a story told.
The sands of time shift ever slow,
Yet seeds of hope begin to grow.

In shards of glass, reflections play,
A dance of shadows, light on display.
Though scattered pieces find their place,
Together weave the dreams we chase.

With every heartbeat, visions rise,
In fragments whispered, the spirit flies.
For in the cracks, we find our way,
To shape a world where dreams can stay.

Footprints on Fresh Soil

In morning light, I tread so soft,
The earth awakens, life aloft.
Each step I take, a trace remains,
A sign of growth, despite the pains.

With every mark, a story told,
Of dreams once timid, now so bold.
The soil embraces, warm and deep,
A memory shared, a promise to keep.

Through fields of green, my path does weave,
In nature's arms, I find reprieve.
The echoes linger, whispers near,
Guiding me onward, casting out fear.

Footprints fading, time moves fast,
Yet in my heart, these moments last.
I leave my mark, and in return,
The soil gives back, and I shall learn.

Songs of the Unseen

In shadows cast, the whispers play,
A melody that guides the day.
The air is thick, with secrets sung,
In every heart, this song is sprung.

A breeze that sways the silent trees,
Carries notes that dance with ease.
Invisible hands weave threads of sound,
In silent spaces, magic found.

With every breath, the rhythm flows,
A symphony that ebbs and grows.
To listen close is to perceive,
The stories woven, we conceive.

These tunes of life, we often miss,
Yet in their silence, lies pure bliss.
For every note unknown, unsung,
The songs of unseen have just begun.

Chasing the Horizon

With every dawn, I chase the light,
The promise held in morning bright.
A journey calls, the road unfolds,
Adventure waits, as dreams are told.

Each step I take, the world reveals,
New vistas born, each turn, it heals.
The sky ablaze, with colors fierce,
In boundless beauty, hearts immerse.

The horizon stretches, beckons me,
A canvas vast, for eyes to see.
I run with hope, my spirit free,
In every chase, I find a key.

Though trails may twist, and paths may bend,
Each moment lives, a means to mend.
So onward still, my spirit flies,
Chasing the horizon, where dreams arise.

A Canvas of Possibilities

On this blank slate, my thoughts collide,
A spectrum bright, where dreams reside.
Each stroke of color, wild and free,
Creating worlds, as hearts can see.

With every hue, a story grows,
An endless muse, where passion flows.
In splatters bold, and lines refined,
Endless visions spill from the mind.

A canvas waiting, bare and wide,
Inviting chaos, joy, and pride.
In every curve, a tale is spun,
Each moment cherished, battles won.

So here I stand, brush in my hand,
To paint the dreams in a vibrant land.
A canvas of life, so rich, so bright,
Filled with possibilities, pure delight.

Unfolding the Future

In the dawn of dreams we rise,
Paths uncharted stretch before our eyes.
Whispers of hope dance in the breeze,
Promising light through the thickest trees.

Each step forward, a choice we make,
With every heartbeat, the world will shake.
Threads of fate weave stories anew,
Building the bridge to what we pursue.

The stars above guide our way,
Lighting the night until the day.
With courage strong, we venture forth,
Embracing the unknown, we find our worth.

Together we seek, hand in hand,
In unity, we make a stand.
For the future unfolds in dreams, it seems,
Crafted by our hearts and our shared themes.

A Symphony of Small Things

Each raindrop sings a gentle tune,
The rustling leaves sway to the moon.
A child's laughter, a fleeting sound,
Echoes of joy that linger around.

In quiet moments, beauty grows,
A fragrant bloom in a world that knows.
Small gestures spark, ignite the air,
Reminders that love is everywhere.

The whispered tales of day's retreat,
Every heartbeat a rhythmic beat.
A warm embrace when shadows fall,
A symphony of small things calls.

Let us cherish the world so near,
In tiny wonders, we hold dear.
For in the simple lies a grace,
A melody of life we all can trace.

Awakening Shadows

In twilight's hush, the shadows creep,
Whispers of secrets the night will keep.
With every thought, they stretch and sway,
Inviting us to join their play.

Beneath the stars, stories arise,
In the quiet dark, wisdom lies.
An echo of dreams that softly blend,
Awakening whispers that never end.

Through misty paths we slowly tread,
Facing the fears that lingered in bed.
Yet courage blooms in the dead of night,
As shadowed figures step into light.

With dawn's first breath, the shadows fade,
Revealing the truths the night portrayed.
In every ending, a new chance to find,
The beauty of change in the heart and mind.

Blossoms of Change

In the garden where the wildflowers stand,
Petals unfold, soft as a hand.
Colors burst forth, vibrant and bright,
A tapestry woven in morning light.

With every season, new life takes flight,
Transforming the earth in shades of delight.
Roots intertwine, forming a bond,
As nature reclaims what we have donned.

Change is a cycle, a rhythmic dance,
Each bloom a story, each leaf a chance.
For in the shift lies hope anew,
Blossoms of change in every hue.

Let hearts remember through all we face,
Every ending leads to a sacred place.
Together we grow, in sun and in rain,
Embracing the beauty in blossoms of change.

Shimmering Possibilities

In the dawn's soft glow, dreams awake,
Whispers of hope in breezes shake.
A canvas of wishes, colors bright,
Painted with warmth, kissed by light.

Every choice leads down a road,
Where flowers of fate in silence explode.
The heart feels a pull, a gentle sway,
Guiding us forth, come what may.

Stars above guide with their gleam,
Flickering softly, igniting a dream.
In shadows of doubt, courage will rise,
Embracing the light that never denies.

So dance in the moments, let spirits soar,
Trust in the journey, and seek evermore.
In shimmering possibilities, we find our way,
A tapestry woven, brightening day.

Serene Unfolding

In the quiet hour, calmness reigns,
Gentle breezes weave through lanes.
A soft whisper flows through the trees,
Nature's embrace, a soothing breeze.

Petals unfurl in the morning light,
Colors emerge, a beautiful sight.
Each moment lingers, sacred and pure,
Inviting the heart to softly endure.

As shadows dance with the fading sun,
A peaceful sigh says the day is done.
With stars above, the night takes hold,
A cozy blanket of darkness, bold.

In serene unfolding, life finds its grace,
Time slows down, a tender space.
We breathe and bask in the quiet tune,
Under the watch of the silver moon.

Fragile New Directions

Tender whispers in the night,
Guide us to paths of soft light.
In fragile moments, courage grows,
Towards the unknown, the heart bravely goes.

Each step taken is a chance,
A dance with fate, a gentle glance.
In the fragility, strength is found,
Rising like flowers from the ground.

The world spins full of choices anew,
Embracing the change, we find what's true.
With each heartbeat, the future unfolds,
Stories unwritten await to be told.

In fragile new directions, we dare to dream,
Navigating life's ever-changing stream.
With open hearts and minds so free,
We tread the path of what can be.

Cascading Waves of Insight

With each wave that breaks on shore,
Comes the wisdom of tales before.
Cascades of thoughts, they ebb and flow,
Revealing secrets only the sea can know.

In the rush of tides, we hear the call,
Echoes of truth that rise and fall.
Each splash carries lessons, old and wise,
Reflecting the skies in changing guise.

Beneath the surface, depths invite,
A journey inward, a search for light.
In the calm between the storm's embrace,
Insights shimmer in a sacred space.

As we ride these waves of thought and dream,
We find our purpose, and a deeper theme.
In cascading waves, our spirits unite,
Illuminating paths in the quiet of night.

The Bloom of Resolve

In gardens where the brave do tread,
Seeds of will begin to spread.
From the soil of trials past,
A strength emerges, unsurpassed.

With each dawn, the petals rise,
Chasing dreams beneath the skies.
Resilient hearts in silence grow,
A beauty only few can know.

Through storms and shadows, firm they stand,
With roots that grasp the fertile land.
For every tear, a blossom bright,
Transforms the dark into pure light.

And so they flourish, bold and free,
These blooms of hope, a sight to see.
In every heart, a promise calls,
Where courage blooms, love never falls.

Kindling the Spark

From the ashes, embers glow,
A flicker waits to break the snow.
With a breath, the flame ignites,
Illuminating hidden nights.

Ideas dance like fireflies,
Swirling through the open skies.
In hearts where passion starts to rise,
A spark ignites, the spirit flies.

With every strike, the fire grows,
Forging paths where courage flows.
In the warmth, new visions gleam,
Turning whispers into dreams.

So gather round, let's feed the blaze,
Together in this fiery haze.
For in the spark, our futures lie,
As bright as stars that paint the sky.

Echoes of Ambition

In valleys deep, ambitions call,
Resounding echoes, one and all.
With every heartbeat, dreams take flight,
Guiding souls through the darkest night.

Voices rise from shadows cast,
Whispers of triumph from the past.
Chasing visions, bold and clear,
Each echo fuels a growing cheer.

Through mountains high and rivers wide,
The echoes of our dreams abide.
With every step, the journey molds,
A story penned that never folds.

United by these distant cries,
We reach for stars that light our skies.
In every echo, hope resides,
As ambition guides our rising tides.

Winds of New Directions

When the winds begin to change,
Paths unfold, life feels so strange.
With gentle whispers, they invite,
To sail beyond the known daylight.

Through valleys lush and skies anew,
The winds awaken dreams in you.
Carrying hopes on silver wings,
In every gust, a promise sings.

As seasons shift, the heart will learn,
To bend and sway, to twist and turn.
In every breeze, a lesson found,
Where courage rises from the ground.

So take a breath and feel the air,
Embrace the change, shed every care.
For in these winds, our lives ignite,
A journey launched towards the light.

Whispering Intentions

In shadows soft, intentions breathe,
Chasing dreams, beyond belief.
A silence speaks, a secret sigh,
As hopes take wing, they learn to fly.

Through rustling leaves, the wishes grow,
In twilight hues, their colors glow.
Each heartbeat drums, a steady call,
With whispered thoughts, we rise, we fall.

Embrace the night, let stillness reign,
In the quiet, we feel no pain.
The stars above, they nod with grace,
To every soul that seeks a place.

With gentle hands, we shape the clay,
Molding paths, to guide our way.
The universe aligns, responds,
To whispered dreams that flow like ponds.

Changeling Footprints

In secret woods, where shadows creep,
The changelings dance where spirits leap.
Each footprint left, a tale to spin,
Of magic lost and found within.

Through shifting paths, the echoes call,
They weave a web around us all.
In moonlit glades, their laughter rings,
A melody of ancient things.

Wings brush against the midnight air,
With every shift, we shed despair.
The world transforms, begins anew,
As changeling souls find purpose true.

A fleeting glance, a knowing smile,
We wander free, if just a while.
In every step, a story stirs,
The magic waits, it softly purrs.

Rewriting Routines

Change the script, and break the mold,
From worn-out paths, we now grow bold.
Routine fades, in evening's glow,
As new rhythms begin to flow.

With every dawn, a chance to start,
To reimagine the child's heart.
In simple acts, we redefine,
The beauty found in moments fine.

Turn left instead of going right,
Embrace the spark that feels so bright.
Each step we take, a fresh delight,
In twilight hours, we feel the light.

Unraveled threads create new seams,
As life unfolds, we chase our dreams.
The dance evolves, a sweet refrain,
In rewriting ways, we find our gain.

Gentle Revolutions

Whispers in the air, a soft refrain,
Awakening hearts, igniting change.
With every breath, a spark ignites,
In quiet strength, we find our might.

Gentle hands, they mold the clay,
Transforming fear into the day.
In shared intentions, we unite,
To cast away the endless night.

The tides may rise, but we stand firm,
With hope as fuel, our spirits burn.
Together we rise, a brand-new song,
In gentle revolutions, we belong.

Embrace the soft, the power found,
In patient steps on sacred ground.
With hearts aligned, our voices soar,
In gentle revolutions, we explore.

Mosaic of Moments

In whispers of time we find,
Each second a piece, intertwined.
Colors of laughter, shades of tears,
Every heartbeat echoes through years.

Fragments of joy, sorrow, and grace,
Together they form a sacred space.
Each memory shines, a delicate thread,
In the fabric of life, where all is said.

Sunrise and sunset dance in our mind,
Treasures of moments, rare and unconfined.
A fleeting glimpse of what we hold dear,
In the mosaic of life, we persevere.

With every new day, a chance to embrace,
The art of existence, a beautiful trace.
We gather the pieces, both bright and dim,
Creating a life that sings from within.

Chasing the Light

Through shadows we wander, hearts open wide,
In search of the glow, where dreams can collide.
With every step forward, we aim for the sky,
A dance with the dawn, as we learn how to fly.

The sun paints the horizon, a canvas aglow,
Illuminating paths where we long to go.
With hope as our compass, we navigate night,
Chasing the brilliance, embracing the light.

In moments of silence, we find clarity's spark,
As shadows retreat, revealing the dark.
We rise with the stars, a symphony bright,
Forever in motion, we're chasing the light.

With hearts full of wonder, we stand at the brink,
Exploring the depths, learning how to think.
In the glow of the future, our spirits take flight,
Together we journey, forever in light.

Breathing in Possibility

Each inhale a promise, a world yet to see,
Exhaled are the doubts that once wanted to be.
With every soft breath, we claim our own space,
Igniting the spark, embracing the grace.

A canvas of chances, colored in dreams,
The universe whispers in delicate streams.
We dance to the rhythm of what could unfold,
In the realm of potential, our stories are told.

With visions unbounded, we leap into the vast,
Eagerly tasting the future, unsurpassed.
The air filled with promise, electric and bright,
Breathing in possibility, igniting the night.

With hearts wide open, we welcome the flow,
Eyes searching afar for what we can sow.
In the garden of wonder, we tend to our plight,
Breathing in hope, we reach for the light.

A Tapestry of Tomorrow

Woven together, each thread a bright hue,
Stitching our futures, in colors so true.
With hands full of dreams, we craft our desire,
In the loom of existence, we build and aspire.

The fabric of moments, both fragile and strong,
Chosen with care, to create our own song.
In the chorus of life, each voice finds its place,
Together we flourish, in unity and grace.

With visions of hope, we lay the foundation,
A structure of purpose, beyond limitation.
Threading the past with the dreams of today,
We stitch a tomorrow, in our own unique way.

As we weave through the challenges, laughter and tears,
Embracing the journey that steers us through years.
With every new dawn, we continue to sow,
This tapestry of tomorrow, where dreams overflow.

Awakening the Dawn

Soft whispers call the light,
As shadows fade from sight.
The earth begins to stir,
In hues of gold, a blur.

Birdsong dances on the breeze,
Stirring leaves upon the trees.
With each ray, a promise made,
New beginnings, unafraid.

Clouds dissolve in morning's grace,
Every heartbeat finds its place.
Hope ignites the waking sky,
In this moment, we all fly.

Awakening the day ahead,
With dreams that never go unsaid.
In this light, we find our way,
Embracing all that comes our way.

Seeds of Change

In silence, whispers grow,
From tiny seeds, a flow.
Roots reach deep beneath the ground,
In their strength, hope is found.

Gentle hands will scatter wide,
Planting dreams that will not hide.
Watered by the tears we shed,
New paths sprout where fears have led.

Each leaf a story yet to tell,
Of trials fought and all we fell.
Through struggle, blossoms we see,
A vivid world, wild and free.

With every harvest, change we yield,
A tapestry that can be healed.
Together, we will rearrange,
The beauty born from seeds of change.

The Art of Tomorrow

Canvas stretched beneath our dreams,
Splashing color, bright beams.
Each stroke an echo of our fears,
Creating visions through the years.

With every brush, we carve the scene,
A dance of shadows, bright and keen.
In the chaos, form appears,
A masterpiece born from our tears.

Moments weave with threads of fate,
In this gallery, we create.
Timeless visions we will find,
Expressions painted, heart and mind.

The art we craft, tomorrow's grace,
A legacy in every space.
With passion, we reshape our story,
In waves of hope, we find our glory.

Gentle Shifts

In stillness, change, a soft caress,
Like whispers woven, we progress.
The world spins in quiet sighs,
As each moment lightly flies.

Little things, they take their time,
Building dreams, a subtle climb.
Ripples spread from small to grand,
Guiding hearts with gentle hands.

See how light transforms the night,
As stars reveal their hidden light.
Each shift, a chance to renew,
A landscape slowly breaks in two.

In the dawn of every change,
We embrace the grand exchange.
With open hearts, we stand to lift,
The beauty found in gentle shifts.

Navigating the Turn

In the dusk of decision, we stand,
With winding paths before us, unseen.
Each choice like a current, a guiding hand,
Pulling us closer to what might have been.

The compass of dreams whispers softly,
Tracking the twists of fate along the way.
In shadows of doubt, we strive boldly,
To find the light in the heart of the fray.

A map of the moments we hold dear,
Drawing lines through the moments of pain.
With courage, we let go of our fear,
Embracing the journey, come what may.

The turn is a promise, a chance to grow,
With every step forward, we weave our tale.
Leaves of the past, like rivers, must flow,
To navigate the turn, we must set sail.

Fresh Pages Turned

In the quiet of morning, new chapters await,
The ink of intention starts to flow.
Blank pages beckon, a canvas of fate,
With whispers of stories yet to bestow.

Each sunrise heralds a turn of the pen,
Words waiting, eager to breathe and ignite.
In the dance of creation, we play once again,
Crafting our dreams in the soft morning light.

The ink spills over with hopes held tight,
Colors of life splashed in bold, vibrant hues.
Every line a promise, a flicker of light,
Unraveling tales that we choose to pursue.

Turning fresh pages, the future draws near,
Each moment a verse, a song to be sung.
In the rhythm of living, we conquer our fear,
With every new story, we stay forever young.

Reimagining the Ordinary

In the humdrum of days, we seek the bright,
Finding magic in moments we often miss.
A simple glance can ignite delight,
Transforming the mundane into bliss.

Laughter lives in the spaces between,
Where hearts connect in a tender embrace.
Every breath a reminder, a gentle sheen,
Revealing the beauty in a familiar place.

Through the lens of wonder, we start to see,
The extraordinary in the everyday grind.
Like leaves dancing in a soft summer breeze,
Imagination awakens, igniting the mind.

So let us cherish the ordinary glow,
With eyes wide open, we craft our own way.
In the dance of simplicity, we flourish and grow,
Reimagining life with each passing day.

Daring to Dream Again

In the shadow of silence, dreams start to stir,
Whispers of hope rising, soft like the dawn.
With courage igniting, we dare and prefer,
To chase after wishes, like birds newly drawn.

Brushed by the winds of the past, we arise,
Unfolding our wings in the light of the sun.
With each gentle heartbeat, our spirit complies,
In the realm of the daring, new journeys begun.

The canvas is vast, with colors unspooled,
Tonight we are artists, reclaiming our right.
With laughter like paint, our fears are untooled,
Daring to flourish, to dream through the night.

A tapestry woven from threads of our fall,
In the fabric of life, resilience shines bright.
With hearts reawakened, we answer the call,
Daring to dream again, we embrace the night.

The Dance of Consistency

In the quiet of the night, we sway,
With every step, we find our way.
A rhythm steady, hearts aligned,
In the dance of life, peace we find.

Through storms that try to break the chain,
We hold our ground, we rise again.
The echoes of our steadfast grace,
In every twirl, we find our place.

The world may change, and seasons shift,
Yet in our hearts, we hold the gift.
Consistency, our silent song,
In the dance of life, we all belong.

Together in the quiet night,
We'll weave our dreams, bathed in light.
With every step, we take our stand,
In unity, we make our plan.

Threads of Renewal

Soft whispers of the morning dew,
Awakening the earth anew.
Each leaf unfurls, each bud will bloom,
In nature's arms, there's always room.

Woven in time, the stories told,
Threads of renewal, bright and bold.
From ashes rise, we learn to grow,
In every struggle, seeds we sow.

The sun will rise, the shadows fade,
With each new dawn, our fears are laid.
In vibrant colors, life will dance,
As we embrace this second chance.

With gentle hands and hopeful hearts,
We stitch together a brand new start.
Threads of renewal, strong and fine,
Together we'll craft a life divine.

Pages Turning

In the quiet of the evening light,
We turn the pages, hearts alight.
Each chapter holds a tale untold,
Whispers of dreams, both shy and bold.

With every flick, a moment's grace,
New voices breathe in this sacred space.
The ink of life, forever flows,
In the depths of silence, wisdom grows.

As stories blend, the past and now,
We learn to cherish, to take a bow.
In each new line, a lesson learned,
As the fire within us steadily burned.

So let us write with laughter's song,
In the book of life, where we belong.
Each page we turn, a step to take,
In this journey, each breath we make.

Metamorphosis at Dawn

In the hush before the daybreak sound,
Life stirs softly from the ground.
With colors bright, the sky ignites,
A canvas fresh, a true delight.

From the cocoon, a butterfly soars,
Embracing change, it freely roars.
With every flap, old fears subside,
In this rebirth, we find our pride.

The sun will rise, the shadows flee,
In the metamorphosis, we are free.
Each moment's gift, a chance to grow,
In the light of dawn, our spirits glow.

So let us welcome this new embrace,
A journey shared, we find our place.
Metamorphosis at the break of day,
With open hearts, we find our way.

Sails Set for Destiny

With sails unfurled, we chase the sun,
Each wave a whisper, a journey begun.
The horizon beckons, a tale to unfold,
In the dance of the tides, our dreams take hold.

Guided by stars, in the night so bright,
We navigate paths, with hearts full of light.
The winds of fortune, they carry us far,
To lands unknown, where the wild things are.

Each gust a promise, each swell a chance,
We'll journey onward, in fate's embrace dance.
Together we'll wander, side by side,
With sails set high, we'll make the world wide.

As dawn breaks softly, the future we see,
With courage we sail, forever we'll be.
Our destiny calls, we answer its plea,
With sails set for adventure, wild and free.

Navigating the New Dawn

A new day rises, the sky ablaze,
With colors vibrant, in a joyful haze.
We chart our course through the morning mist,
In the heart of the light, dreams still persist.

Our compass points toward the vast unknown,
With hope as our anchor, we've fully grown.
Each step we take on this path brand new,
Unfolding like petals, kissed by the dew.

Through fields of possibility, we wander wide,
With strength and vision, we won't subside.
Together we'll face any storm that's near,
In unity's bond, we'll conquer our fear.

With laughter as music, we'll not be bound,
In harmony's rhythm, our joy is found.
As daylight rises, the world sings along,
In navigating dawn, we find where we belong.

Artistry of the Present

In moments fleeting, beauty unfolds,
A canvas of life painted in gold.
Each breath a brush stroke, a masterpiece spun,
In the artistry present, we dance as one.

Colors of laughter, shades of our tears,
Crafting a story through all of our years.
With passion ignited, we capture the now,
In the tapestry of time, we make our vow.

Letting go gently of what came before,
Embracing each second, forever in store.
We savor the warmth of each fleeting glance,
In the artistry woven, we take our chance.

Each heartbeat a rhythm, alive with the thrill,
We paint with intention, with strength and with will.
In the gallery of life, we find our own way,
In the artistry present, we seize every day.

Phoenix Rising

From ashes we rise, a flame ignites,
With wings spread wide, we embrace new heights.
In trials we forged, our spirits reborn,
A phoenix at dawn, our fears now outworn.

With light in our hearts, we soar through the air,
Adventuring boldly, casting away care.
Each challenge a spark, igniting our fire,
A testament true to our growing desire.

Through storms we've emerged, with wisdom we've gained,
An unbreakable spirit that won't be contained.
The essence of strength, in our souls it resides,
Like a phoenix in flight, our hope never hides.

In the warmth of the sun, we find our rebirth,
Celebrating life, embracing our worth.
With wings that can conquer the vast open skies,
We rise once again, as the phoenix who flies.

Colors of Change

In the dawn, hues start to blend,
A palette fresh, where shadows mend.
Emerald leaves sway with grace,
While skies wear blue, a broad embrace.

Golden rays peek through the trees,
Whispers carried by the breeze.
Scarlet blooms adorn the ground,
In each moment, beauty found.

The world transforms with every breath,
Each shade a dance, defying death.
Twilight paints in softest light,
A canvas rich, dark turns to bright.

At day's end, colors fade away,
Yet in our hearts, they come to stay.
A cycle vast, forever spins,
In colors of change, life begins.

Touchstones of Transformation

On the path, we find our way,
Each stone whispers what to say.
Footprints mark where we have tread,
Guiding us where dreams are fed.

With each step, a lesson learned,
In the fire, our spirits burned.
Rivers flow, change finds its course,
Unfolding life with gentle force.

In the silence, echoes call,
Stories rise and softly fall.
Boundless sky, our hopes take flight,
In every dark, we seek the light.

These touchstones show the way we grow,
Through trials faced and seeds we sow.
A journey shaped by love and grace,
In transformation, we find our place.

A Symphony of Steps

With every step, a note is played,
In life's great dance, we are arrayed.
Feet on ground, hearts in tune,
Underneath the watchful moon.

The rhythm calls, the tempo starts,
As laughter flows from eager hearts.
In this ballet, joy prevails,
As we compose our vibrant tales.

Syncopated beats of chance,
In the moment, we find romance.
A waltz of dreams, we intertwine,
Creating music, pure, divine.

Through valleys low and peaks so high,
Our symphony, it'll never die.
Each step, a line in our refrain,
In this grand dance, love will remain.

Reimagined Yesterdays

In the mirror, shadows stare,
Fragments of a world laid bare.
Echoes from the paths we roamed,
Whispers of a life, well-homed.

Turning pages, stories unfold,
Lessons learned, in daring bold.
Past reflections shimmer bright,
Guiding us toward the light.

Colors fade, but memories stay,
Each heartbeat, a soft replay.
From ashes rise, we start anew,
With courage sewn in every hue.

Reimagined, we carve our fate,
Taking steps that motivate.
In the canvas of our days,
Yesterdays, redefined, we blaze.

Aligning the Stars

In the hush of night, they gleam,
Whispers of fate, guiding the dream.
Connect the dots in the vast expanse,
A cosmic dance, a fateful chance.

Hope flickers bright, a beacon in dark,
Each twinkle a wish, a vital spark.
Charting the course on celestial seas,
Aligning the stars with gentle ease.

Moments converge in a splendid glow,
Paths intertwine where the heartbeats flow.
The universe weaves tales of old,
A tapestry rich, a sight to behold.

Breathe in the magic, let it unfold,
For destiny waits, both brave and bold.
With every step on this endless quest,
Aligning the stars, we find our rest.

Tapestry of Tomorrows

Threads of color, woven tight,
Stories of old, whispers of light.
Every stitch a hope or dream,
In the fabric of life, we find our theme.

Waves of time in patterns flow,
Guiding us gently where we must go.
Each choice a pixel in the grand display,
A tapestry bright, come what may.

The loom of life is wide and grand,
With every heartbeat, we take a stand.
Knots of struggle, laughter, and tears,
Crafting our futures, confronting our fears.

Embrace the colors, let them unite,
Creating a vision, a beacon of light.
In this tapestry, we all play a part,
A journey of tomorrows, sewn with the heart.

Silhouettes of Self-Discovery

In the shadows, the truth resides,
Shapes of self where the heart confides.
Drawn in light, but shaded by doubt,
Silhouettes dance, revealing the route.

With every step, a layer peels,
Unveiling wounds, the heart it heals.
Journey within, through valleys and heights,
Discovering self in the quiet nights.

Echoes of laughter, whispers of pain,
Each mark and scar, a wisdom gain.
Fluid and free, we shape our fate,
In shadows' embrace, we illuminate.

Find beauty in flaws, the imperfect grace,
In silhouettes formed, we find our place.
With every heartbeat, the truth becomes clear,
Self-discovery's dance, our soul's frontier.

Breaking the Mold

In the confines of rigid frames,
Dare to rise, ignite the flames.
Shatter the glass with a fearless heart,
Embrace the chaos, let it start.

Whispers of doubt fade in the roar,
With every step, we seek for more.
No longer bound by what they say,
Breaking the mold, we're here to stay.

The winds of change swirl in the night,
Carrying dreams that take to flight.
Cast aside limits, stretch your wings,
Discover the joy that true freedom brings.

In the tapestry of life, stand bold,
With colors anew, our stories told.
Breaking the mold, we find our way,
A symphony of selves, we proudly play.

Milton Keynes UK
Ingram Content Group UK Ltd.
UKHW020936041024
449263UK00011B/557